Andie invites the reader into a : raw places of her life story as a: of God in her life. If you are a her story will confirm that the : and redeemer of the lost. If you are a new ~~~~ ~ be drawn into discovery and exploration of the many facets of the God who created you so intentionally. Expect to be encouraged, inspired, and compelled to be used by God for His purposes.

—Shirley Charles-Robinson,

Author of *Heart's Cry: Made with Purpose For A Purpose* and podcast host of Purposeful Living

Touching to the core, Andie Alama-Smith's, *Beautified Brokenness*, illustrates for us the transforming power of God. In this book one can clearly see the sovereign and providential hand of God working in Andie's life and the lives of those around her.

A woman of undying faith, Andie demonstrates what true humility, charity, kindness, and strength looks like. She is a woman who has persevered in her faith through many of life's trails and storms and yet has remained a constant for many who have gone through their own storms.

It is an honor and blessing to know a woman such as herself and read this tear-jerking testimony. Her prayers and love have brought much comfort, healing, and truth in my own life. God is powerfully glorified through this life transforming testimony! I highly recommend this book to anyone who desires a fresh touch from God, a touch of His love. Be ready to encounter the love of God through this powerful testimony!

"And we know that in all things, God works together for the good of those who love Him, who have been called according to His purpose." Romans 8:28, NIV

—Marian Pachanian-Hilmer

Author and Co-Illustrator of *The Brave Little Puppy Finds A Home*, Music Composer, Song Writer, Artist/Worship leader

Romans 1:17, KJV, says, *"For therein is the righteousness of God revealed from faith to faith: as it is written, the just shall live by faith."*

If we look and listen well enough in our lives, we will see the goodness and faithfulness of Jesus Christ on display for all. Of course, just as Romans 1:17 tells us, it requires a man or woman of faith to glorify God and to be glorified by God.

Andie Alama-Smith is an amazing living example of Christ's righteousness revealed, in Christ's faithfulness revealed, and in one woman's journey to serve and live for God in total faith.

I'm excited for everyone who is reading and is going to read Andie's personal testimony and witness of God's work and glory. Not only is it an amazing true story about Christ's amazing grace and hand upon Andie's life; but it's also a compelling true story about a humble, kind, hard-working, and faithful woman of God who has kept the faith through thick and thin. What an opportunity for you, the reader, to see that God is good and to meditate and soak in His righteousness, promises, and goodness.

For those of us who know Andie personally, we can testify to her credibility as a storyteller and as a woman of faith who not only "talks the talk," but also "walks the walk." In my humble opinion, Andie is a true servant of Christ who "practices what she preaches."

In this day and age, it's easy to claim just about anything you want to, and people will believe. Andie Alama Smith is as genuine as they come. I believe this is exactly why God has led her to author this book you are reading today.

Those of us who know Andie, know her story, her heart, and her integrity. What a special treat to all of you that she is sharing this story. God is so good. If you don't know; come and see. Allow Andie to take you on a journey through her life and see that God is not only real, but also faithful and good.

Thank you, Andie, for writing this book and for all you do for The Kingdom.

—Roger Hilmer

All Glory to God – Executive Director

I believe Andie has always shown a commitment to see the glory of Jesus be encountered by hungry hearts. She has served with a faithful heart and drew people closer to each other. Thank you, Andie, for making Jesus our magnificent obsession.

—Ajay Samuel

PIHOP – Associate Director

Andie is an awesome friend and encourager with a huge, beautiful heart. Andie has helped me acknowledge, name, and speak healing into my past. She supports me and directs me to Jesus for my healing. Andie shows us we are gifts and our past wounds do not identify us.

—Johnnie Rosas

PIHOP – The Well Prayer Leader
& Living Waters Coordinator

Beautified *Brokenness*

Andie Alama-Smith

Beautified
Brokenness

Beautified Brokenness

Trilogy Christian Publishers

A Wholly Owned Subsidary of Trinity Broadcasting Network

2442 Michelle Drive

Tustin, CA 92780

For information, address Trilogy Christian Publishing

Rights Department, 2442 Michelle Drive, Tustin, CA 92780.

Trilogy Christian Publishing/ TBN and colophon are trademarks of Trinity Broadcasting Network.

For information about special discounts for bulk purchases, please contact Trilogy Christian Publishing.

Manufactured in the United States of America

10 9 8 7 6 5 4 3 2 1

Library of Congress Cataloging-in-Publication Data is available.

ISBN: 979-8-88738-581-5

ISBN: 979-8-88738-582-2

Dedication

This book is dedicated to you. It is my hope that as you read my journey with what God has done in my life, that my story will encourage you to know that He loves you, and that God's love for you is important to embrace, so that your identity would be found in Him.

You have purpose and are fashioned specifically by God to fulfill His plans. I am truly grateful for the people God has used to shape my life and helped me along the way.

> Love does not delight in evil but rejoices with the truth

> 1 Corinthians 13:6 (NIV)

Acknowledgments

A special thanks extended to my siblings, Josie, Moreli, Gabriel and DJ for supporting me through this journey, my husband Grant for loving me, my niece Alena for your words of encouragement, Ajay who prophesied over me that I'd be writing a book from the PIHOP team, Cheryl and the leadership team from PIHOP, TIRLA from PIHOP, Pastor Matthew and Caroline from The Dream Center, Pastor Rene and Nora from Victory Outreach- Van Nuys, Johnnie from PIHOP and Living Waters, Roger and Marian from All Glory to God for their support and prayers. My cousin Elsie who invited me to church and all my close friends who have loved me unconditionally, as my story is also theirs.

Introduction

It began with a prophecy! Just sitting around a fire-pit at Lois's birthday party - random and small talk conversations lead to prophetic word that stirred my heart to put pen to paper. Within a few days, five chapters were written without any blockage. It was as if the anointing oil was stored in the alabaster jar for many years, waiting to be poured out - and its sweet fragrance flowed with tears of joy and utter sadness. But - I was reminded of my redemption and the power of Yeshua's spirit overwhelmed me to continue putting pen to paper. My story can only be told from the places of brokenness with shattered dreams, to reveal that God alone is the only one who can refine, shape, mold and prosper you into His plans and promises for prosperity. He is enriched with truth and love, and only desires that we know His nature and His heart for fulfilling His dreams. Let His dreams become your dreams – but it must start with using your brokenness for refining.

Prologue

Many say that brokenness is part of life that we cannot avoid. I've broken glasses, fingernails, Christmas ornaments and guitar strings. I've had broken promises, a broken heart and even experienced broken relationships. Brokenness may be something we're familiar with, but it is often misunderstood.

Let's be open to knowing this truth, that because it is all too real and we all do experience it, brokenness is reality that is incapable of denial, raw, part of our human nature experience but a substance that will eventually find a place in God's heart. Your brokenness doesn't define who you are and what you've done. It's a resource that only God can use to bring richness, depth, life, and redemption. Let's be reminded that God is no stranger to our human experience. We can find hope in knowing that our brokenness will bring healing to each other.

Table of Contents

Chapter 1 – Your Name

They say that your name is the most important thing to identify with, that names have meanings, it signifies your purpose, your calling, who you are and what you were designed to be. And if you were ever blessed to have parents who thought about your name, prayed about your name, even discussed your name – then, you know that 'what you were called,' was intentionally thought of with a meaning.

This, however, was not a truth for me – "Andrea," my name was always connected and associated with an emotion of fear, shame, or anger. My mum said she named me after her midwife at the hospital – someone she had only known for a few days. No discussion about it, no research into the meaning, just a decision based on a relationship with a woman she had met.

I had always questioned my purpose, my upbringing, my identity, who I am. But, for you to know my story, you must know my parents. As I write this book, I must confess that I'm discovering more of who I am and why God has called me to place pen to paper, so… here we go.

Both my parents were hard workers, ambitious, and career oriented. Their status and their reputations were very important to them – there is a strength and sense of self-worth when having Samoan pride! Both my parents were born and raised in Upolu Samoa, though their upbringing were very different, the culture of representing your family well and living up to expectations were very similar.

Ester, the eldest of her siblings, nine in total, loved to teach and sing. I don't really know much about her childhood stories, only that she was nineteen years old when she married my father and that she was carrying another man's child. Papa, my grandfather, had recently remarried after grandma passed away, but had dealt with his mourning by drinking alcohol.

I discovered that my great grandma had encouraged mum to either flee the country or marry someone so that the pregnancy would not look like a sin – low and behold, her meeting dad were the answers to her situation – she married dad and moved to New Zealand.

I can only imagine the guilt and shame she would've been carrying, but also anxiety of the secrecy of her pregnancy – dad said he didn't know mum was pregnant until they officially married – they were married within weeks of having met each other.

I remember my parents saying their marriage was arranged and that they had negotiated an agreement to try and make things work between them. Back in the 60's when Samoa became the first Pacific Island state to regain its independence, the New Zealand government offered an opportunity for Samoans to migrate to their country where they were promised a better way of life, and so, many of my parent's generation moved to New Zealand for this reason – to raise their kids and families with provisional promises.

Mum at age nineteen, newly married and filled with hope and wonder, confessed to dad of her pregnancy, but started her career and pursued her dream to be a teacher and community influencer – she successfully graduated with her credentials and degrees and was quickly placed into a role as a primary school teacher.

I'm so proud of mum and all her achievements, she taught me how to pursue your dreams and goals and make sacrifices to pursue it. However, my childhood memories of mum were absent – i.e., "the absence of motherhood." She was always busy, always working, always committed to some committee or organization, gone early in the morning and would return late at night. She did a great job with occupying herself with playing an important role in the community or part of someone else's life, but to me and my siblings, we didn't feel we were important enough.

I remember a time, mum had to leave home and leave urgently but couldn't take me, so she locked me in the bedroom and drove away. I only remember running up to the window and crying, screaming for her to return. Looking back, I understand that what mum was doing made a lot of sense! She was building an empire of pacific islanders to stand up and fight for justice in a country that was seen to be taking advantage of her people, she was building community initiatives and helping other islanders who were struggling to find their way.

Mum was successful in everything she did. She loved on kids at the primary schools, loved on young adults at the community colleges, she wrote children's books and songs, oversaw the pacific island community cultural performances and initiatives, she was a radio host; she even partnered with key leaders in government to ensure constitutions were in place for protection and good causes of the Pacific Island people.

But, when you are kid, and you don't know what's going on or understand the sacrifices your parents made to 'make a difference' – you rebel and the only reasonings you may have as a child are 'she doesn't love me,' 'she doesn't have time for me.' 'I'm not important enough' – aka – neglect.

Many nights, there was so much anger in our household. Our parents were constantly fighting over us and the care of us, money, time, kids, money, time, kids… I can only describe it as violent memories – physical and verbal abuse. Once again, not understanding the dilemma at hand but to witness the beatings, blood stains, black eyes, and screams of our mum, who can never measure up to dad's expectations. Their daily fights and arguments, one way or another would either result in us sleeping in the yellow station wagon at the park down the street, or if mum wasn't home, we kids would be the resort and outlet for dad's anger and frustration. Mum did her best to protect us and would downplay sleeping in the park as "let's go camping."

I know now that mum kept herself busy, not only because she was pursuing her career and loving the community – but she was protecting her reputation and tried her best to avoid coming home to an abusive husband.

When I reflected on her life, she was driven! All our lives are driven when you think about it... I read: "We're driven by guilt – running from regret and hiding shame, we're driven by resentment and anger – holding onto hurts, we're driven by fear – trauma and unrealistic expectations, we're driven by materialism – where if you possess more, you will mean more or be more important, or driven by approval." These are key headers in Rick Warren's book *The Purpose Driven Life*.

I remember when I gave my heart to the Lord, this was the first Christian book I was given, and this chapter challenged me on so many levels. To understand who I am, I needed to understand who my parents were and how their choices and behaviors became part of my lifestyle.

Growing up, I was teased and called names because I was the teacher's daughter... My name "Andrea" was always used as a mockery or used when my parents were angry and yelled. I never did like the sound of my name. So, at age eight, I was adamant that I would only be called "Andie" and addressed as "Andie" – I even told my teachers to call me this name.

Now, at age forty-seven, when people call me "Andrea," the wounds associated with my name no longer hurt and the sound of my name is sweet, but the scars are still there because they were part of my journey.

I've always loved blown glasses, the different designs and shapes. I never knew that there is a process for making these beautiful, crafted glasses – twelve steps as a matter of fact!

"The blowing glass is a technique used in handicrafts. The glasses can be blown Pyrex and recycled. Pyrex glass is more resistant than other glasses. Glass can be recycled as many times as necessary."

And so, this chapter is '**Process 1** – Materials *(broken glass, steel tube, steel table, tweezers)*. God will use whatever state you're in, to be refined, shaped, molded and glorified for HIS glory. Digging deeper into my name, I researched and discovered this truth:

"Andie" "Andrea" is of Greek origin – is "manly, virile." Its definition are as follows:

- *Having characteristics of an adult male*

- *Energetic or forceful such as strength*

- *Brave, courageous, warrior*

How ironic! God knew that my identity would be found in Him. Even when my parents didn't plan for me, even when my father wanted to abort me and mum avoided my dad throughout her pregnancy, God knew that a midwife on Nov 21, 1975, would influence mum to name me after her – 'brave and courageous.'

For no word from God will ever fail.

Luke 1:37 (NIV)

Chapter 2 – Your Choices

When I chose to write this book, I wanted to be sure that everything mentioned would be used to glorify God for what He has done and is doing. The word "choice" can take you into so many directions – the direction of prosperity or destruction, success or failure, joy or despair – you get the drift…

And while I'm still on the topic of disclosing my parents' story, I can honestly say that their choices, both good and bad, shaped and molded my siblings and I for the greater good!

My dad, David, the fourth eldest of his eleven siblings, was raised in a strict family. As a minister's kid, a pastor's kid, it was never easy to meet the expectations of his father. My dad expressed how he felt like an outcast among his siblings, the black sheep, the one they picked on, spoke down too, cursed, and rebuked. He always felt he was never good enough, smart enough or could ever measure up. All his siblings were doctors, pastors, teachers, lawyers, they all held a high esteemed position or role – but not dad – he was a laborer and worked hard with his hands.

Feeling rejected and outnumbered, he had made choices that led to consequences. To this day, dad still carries the burden, guilt, and shame of the choices he had made – but I believe that Yeshua will bring full restoration and healing to him, once and for all before he passes. Dad was and still is, a handsome man – he was quite the catch to the ladies. Unfortunately, the choice he made as a young man, while dating the daughter of another minister, led her to giving birth to a child out of wedlock.

Oh, how it brought shame to the family name! And so, my grandmother graciously decided to adopt dad's daughter as her own. Dad, young, single and full of shame, saw an opportunity to move to New Zealand and bought into the dream of provisional promises. He had met a woman who was apparently 'the love of his life,' they dated, were engaged and over time, won the hearts of my dad's family, and hers.

At that time, he was working as a welder in New Zealand and his fiancé was an airline hostess for Pacific Airlines. Knowing that their soon-to-be wedding date was quickly approaching, they worked long hours and took any overtime shifts where possible.

On January 14, 1970, my dad's fiancé had received a call and was asked if she was available to take a shift for a flight from Samoa to New Zealand. She obviously said yes and called dad and planned for him to pick her up when she landed. Tragically, the plane crashed 400 yards away from the runway, killing her and all on board. A choice she had made took her life – it was tragic!

When dad heard of her passing, he jumped on the first flight back to the islands to identify her body. Dad described this experience as being the most horrific thing you could ever imagine – the stench of the burnt corpses, the screams of the loved ones, and as he walked towards her body at the back of the hospital, he said he trembled with disbelief. When he removed the sheet from her body, she was still beautifully intact, not one single marking on her body however had died from the sudden impact.

This next decision dad made caused the bystanders to watch in disbelief. It was dad's reaction to seeing her body that labeled him 'the crazy man.' Dad called on a minister that happened to be at the hospital and asked the minister to still marry them – he placed a ring on her finger and married her corpse. My dad had just lost the love of his life and in his disbelief reacted in the only way he knew how. When something tragic like this happens to you, there isn't a right way to react – you can only react. My siblings and I believe this tragedy was the tipping point for dad's manic behavior – either extreme depression or extreme anger.

Weeks went by and dad prepared for her funeral. When the time came to return to New Zealand without the love of his life, he walked into a travel agency and behold – he met my nineteen-year-old mum, who is working part-time and secretly carrying a baby. Dad claims it was love at first sight – negotiations take place, arrangements are discussed, plans are made… It's the beginning of two broken people choosing to try and make amends and pursue happiness in amongst their pain, with no idea who they are or about.

We can never understand the direction life takes us – but we need to know that God will always be paving a way and directing us into the greater purposes He has allowed for us to handle. It was selfish for me to think that if it wasn't for his fiancé's passing, my siblings and I wouldn't be alive – but, there is a truth and revelation I discovered, *"Nothing matters more than knowing God's purposes for your life and nothing can compensate for not knowing them"* – *The Purpose Driven Life* – Rick Warren

Paul wrote *"I'm not saying that I have this all together, that I have it made. But I am well on my way, reaching out for Christ, who has so wondrously reached out for me. Friends don't get me wrong: By no means do I count myself an expert in all of this, but I've got my eye on the goal, where God is beckoning us onward—to Jesus. I'm off and running, and I'm not turning back"* Philippians 3:12-14 (MSG).

Process 2 – Temperature: broken glass needs to be placed in the heat at 2,000 degrees to make it malleable (able to be hammered or pressed permanently without breaking or cracking).

Life is too short to choose a path that doesn't bring you to a place of humility. No matter what we go through and what we face, we need to know that during these high temperature moments, God will not allow us to break. All our relationships are designed to nurture us, mold us, and empower us and God sends people in our lives for this very reason.

What God gives you in life, is a gift from God, what you do with that gift, is a gift from you to Him, how you decide and choose should be based on this truth – what are you doing to choose life as a gift for someone?

> Lord, I will remember what you did. Yes, I will remember your miracles long ago. I will spend time thinking about everything you have done. I will consider all your might acts.
>
> Psalms 77:11-12 (NIV)

Chapter 3 – Your Words

"I wish you were never born," "I never wanted you, you were a mistake," "I hate looking at you, you remind me of your mother/father," "You're too fat," "You'll always be a failure" were familiar phrases and words I'd hear throughout my childhood. These harsh phrases were repeated numerous times, that it eventually became natural behavior without a conscious thought. Our daily words and how we would communicate were rooted from hatred, anger, and fear.

Now don't get me wrong, there were some happy moments in our life, but I would say, the majority of my childhood memories were associated with living in fear, anger and abuse.

Having been raised by two people, who were pursuing their careers, trying to make ends meet, put food on the table, broken with their own identity issues and trying to raise four children with what they had. My parents did the best they could with what they had, yet their words became our words – and all our words were rooted from brokenness that spoke death over each other.

However, outside of home, I had yet experienced another form of words that were not from God. "Tootsie, are you ready to go for a ride?" These words were spoken to me every Monday after school when mum was at her teachers' meeting. Mr. Janitor would push the cart down the corridors, and I would always remember hearing the wheels rolling closer and closer to the door. It was fun riding on the cart, and I would watch him collect trash from each room, go out to the main dumpster then return into the school until we reached our last destination – his storeroom. He would always lift me up onto the high table and tell me to look out the window.

I never knew what violation felt like – at age eight – how could you? As I grew older, Mr. Janitor stopped offering me a ride on his cart. I learned later in life that I was one of the many girls he had sexually abused at our school – I grew out of the feeling of not being special to him anymore because – he had moved onto another victim.

But words, oh how powerful it can be! Our Lord God just spoke His words and created all of creation. No matter how you say it, with your tone, rate of speech, volume or emphasis, your words are a form of a 'love language.'

This is my love language – 'Words of Affirmation.' Whether spoken softly, secretly or harshly, it's what you say that causes me to either respond or react. Over the years I feel I've learnt a lot of effective ways to handle rebuke, misunderstandings, abuse, put downs, negativity etc. I've become a great communicator in reacting with 'comebacks,' abrupt responses, quick remarks, fiery sarcastic comments and even solutions. I've always been told, "You always have something to say!"

However, why is it hard for me to receive a compliment and even respond to a compliment? Shouldn't this be easier to respond to? Especially if my love language is 'words of affirmation?' In the areas of acknowledging kindness and compliments – I know for a fact that this area of my life needs work. I can give words of affirmation and compliments, but it's hard for me to receive. There could possibly be an underlying area of distrust associated with compliments... Mum always promised to take us to McDonalds but never did or other promises she'd make but never kept. Now that I think and write about it, that's got to be it!

I read "one of the most important aspects of 'words of affirmation,' however, is being genuine with these words. People whose primary language is words of affirmation are most about the intentions and emotions behind the words. If you're saying things just to say them, the person will be keen to that. So don't fake it! You don't need to be Romeo, professing your love from the streets below. Be you. Be real. Words such as:

- *"I just want to let you know how proud of you I am."*

- *"You work really hard for us and even when things may feel tough, I just want you to know how appreciative I am."*

- *"I am here if you need me, and I want to help support you in any way I can."*

- *"You're doing such a great job. I'm proud of you."*

- *"Wow, you look so good! I really love the new outfit! It looks great on you."*

I don't remember hearing any of these phrases when I was growing up… ever! And yet, during the season of discovering who I am as a new believer in Christ, I attend a class that assesses your spiritual gifts. Ironically my gift is 'Exhortation.'

> *"The gift of 'Exhortation is often called the 'gift of encouragement.' The Greek word is 'Parakeleo.' It means to seek, exhort, call upon, to encourage and to strengthen.*
>
> *The primary means of exhortation is to remind the hearer of the powerful and amazing work of God in Christ, particularly in regard to the saving work of Jesus in the atonement. The Spirit of God gives the gift to people in church, to strengthen and encourage those who are wavering in their faith. Those with the gift of exhortation can uplift and motivate others, as well as challenge and rebuke them in order to foster spiritual growth and action. The goal of the encourager is to see everyone in the church continually building up the body of Christ*

and glorifying God."- Spiritualgiftstest.com/spiritual-gift-exhortation

Romans 12:8, Acts 11:23-24, 14:21-22, 15:32

Step 3 – Molding - The hot mass of glass is cast into a steel plate to mold and give it a semi-cylindrical shape to the mass.

It is no wonder how God uses all things for His glory and purpose – the lack of love I felt in my upbringing with toxic words and broken promises, has become the actual gift God has instilled in me to use, as a renewed woman of God, saved by grace, exhorting his name, encouraging all and to build up the body of Christ. He has been shaping me and molding me into His likeness.

If you need to speak, speak with intention, love, and purpose. Be real and mindful of the person receiving these words. And if your words won't encourage, either hold your tongue or let it be few. A hard realization to do, even for me – but hey, we're all a work in progress.

> Go ahead and give God thanks for all the glorious things he has done! Give praise to the Lord and announce who he is. Tell the nations what he has done.
>
> Psalms 105:1 (NIV)

Chapter 4 –
Your Dreams

During the time mum was absent at home, I became familiar with her schedule. I knew that after school she had another commitment, so while dad was working late, I would sneak into their room and go into her closet, pulling out all the outfits she had sown as costumes.

Mum was amazing at sowing clothes; it was one of her favorite hobbies she'd do on Saturdays. She had a way of sewing elegant, formal, and bridal-like dresses in many colors. It was one of my favorite memories of things to do when our parents weren't home.

I loved playing dress up and would prance around their bedroom with her platform shoes or 70's high heels. I had friends at school but never had a play friend to come home with and my siblings were doing their own thing, so, I imagined people during my playtime and thoroughly enjoyed the world I was in, conversing with these imaginary people in this false reality.

My brother often teased me saying "Andie, are you talking to yourself again?" Yep, I guess I was! Lol. However, I don't think I ever had a dream or held onto a dream or desire to be anything specific. I would imagine I was an adult who was happier and lived in a happier home and was filled with joy and laughter.

I remember a moment where I gazed at myself in the mirror, I was wearing an oversized dress, heels I couldn't balance on and had said to myself, I want to be different from my parents. I want to be happy and make people laugh and be filled with joy, be the one who has funny jokes and a sense of humor.

For me, that moment changed a part of who I was and my personality. I was known as the clown of the class and became popular for making people laugh. My parents and siblings however, called me 'cheeky' or 'smart mouth.'

Mum nicknamed me "Mickey Mouse." I didn't know why, but I wasn't bothered by her nickname at all, because whenever she called me this, she would laugh, and it would bring joy to her. In writing this book, remember what I had mentioned earlier, I'm discovering myself more, simply by putting pen to paper – I googled Mickey Mouse and here is what came up.

En.wikipedia.org-wiki-mickey-mouse:

"Mickey Mouse is an animated cartoon character who typically wears red shorts, large yellow shoes, and white gloves. Despite being small and vulnerable, Mickey overcomes larger-than-life adversity, through quick wit and a can-do spirit"

Woah! Tears are rolling down my cheeks as I write this character trait about Mickey – oh how mum saw this character trait in me!

God always has a way of revealing goodness in our lives. Even when our dreams were never imagined or if they were robbed/ stolen. He has a way of placing these truths and identity traits of Himself within you. I've only wanted to be surrounded by hope and security and we can only ever experience this with God.

Whatever it looks like at the time, situations and circumstances that are out of our control, I've learnt it's how we respond that matters. Yes, it hurts during the time, yes, it's frustrating to face this, yes, it's unbearable! But when we believe that God has a master plan, He will always carry you through the situation. His breakthrough will manifest when you give it all to Him. Just like climbing a steep hill or mountain peak, it hurts when you're climbing and you must endure the walking up, be disciplined in the areas of endurance, but through it all – He will sustain you as you maintain your faith in God.

Joseph is a great example of someone who was given a dream and he had the ability to interpret dreams – yet his own siblings rebuked him, was thrown into a pit and he was sold into slavery. He held onto a dream God had given him and didn't lose faith. Joseph became the Pharaohs right hand man, second to the king but he was persecuted, incarcerated, betrayed and isolated. His ability to interpret dreams however, catapulted him into a season of prosperity and honor, despite the oppression.

Process 4 – Expanding The air is being blown through a tube to begin expanding the hot mass of glass.

One truth that resonates with me is that there is a difference between happiness and joy. Happiness is emotional and depends on external factors whilst joy is a choice purposefully made. Joy is in the heart, happiness is on the face, joy is of the soul, happiness is of the moment.

God desires that we experience his joy and that our hearts, mind, and spirits be expanded in a way that can only He breathes into us with His unfailing love.

I love the emoji smiley faces – it's always been my signature, on cards, letters, emails, social media... I even have a stress ball 'poopie with a smiley' face on the dashboard of my car. I picked this up at a Small Business Expo, where the small print on the back says, "We get xxxx done."

I can totally relate to this phrase because I, like Mickey Mouse, have a 'can-do spirit.' But there is also another perspective when I look at this emoji – when we feel like crap or when it's hitting the fan... smile! Because even though you feel squeezed like the stress ball, you should know it'll eventually pass, and your breakthrough is on its way!

If God has placed a dream in your heart, don't let it go! It'll happen when you're ready to receive it and walk in it. If you try to make it happen without God's resources and direction, you're only going to be robbing yourself from the blessings He has already prepared for you. Dreams with prosperity are attached to God anyways… let him orchestrate the planning and the resources for you – he doesn't need your help! ☺

When I'm afraid, I put my trust in you.

Psalms 56:3 (NIV)

Chapter 5 – Your Strongholds

This chapter must mention some deep dark things that are not of God – though I don't identify myself as any of these, it was still an experience I had lived and part of who I was at that time in my life.

Now, in my teens, I'm still trying to fit in – I'm hanging out with the boys, a tomboy and trying to find my place of acceptance. A childhood memory of sitting on my dad's lap and being told that I was a mistake, he didn't plan for me, and he'd prefer a boy instead of a girl would never leave my thoughts and were ingrained as part of my so called 'value system.'

For as long as I could remember, we as a family were attending a multicultural Presbyterian Church in Wellington - our first introduction to learning about God, Jesus, and religion. Mum and dad tried hard to ensure that we were not the gossip topic, but you could always feel and sense the tension when our family would walk in. You could even hear the whispers of people muttering behind us when we were told to sit at the front of the church, directly behind them.

We had some great childhood friends and were accepted as part of this island community of young adults, who like all islander families were finding their place and purpose in life. As a teenage islander, we knew the pressure of needing to do well, getting good grades in school, prepare to go to university, be a good example and positive contributor to society – all of these listed above. Besides, this was the reason our parents migrated to New Zealand in the first place – right? The sacrifices they made were constantly reminded to us daily, that we need to represent the family well.

Well, again this wasn't a reality for me or my siblings. The pressure and the expectations had led us in dabbling with either drugs or alcohol to suppress our emotions. I puffed my first cigarette at age thirteen, took my first drink of alcohol at age fourteen, and quickly discovered a group of friends who wanted to experience this lifestyle as rebellious teens. I knew that going to school was important, but not important enough for me. It was my routine of hanging out with my friends, playing sports, and wagging classes to either drink or stay away from home.

My parents knew of my rebellious behavior, but did they know? They didn't know that I lost my virginity at age fifteen to a bass player. I was good at hiding my behaviors, trying to be good at home and behave at church – who would know?

I'd lie and tell mum and dad that I was sleeping over at my friend's place – there was some truth to it, we were having a sleepover, but it was not her house. We girls were dating a group of guys who played in the band – I dated the bass player; she dated the guitarist – you get my drift… and we would always be with them at their gigs at the local pubs, drinking and partying.

My teen years were getting out of control – even dad had enough of me! At age seventeen, not knowing the specifics of why this happened, but I just remember that dad and I argued, I answered him back and he charged at me with a knife. When I fell back onto the bed, my sister jumped in between us to protect me from getting stabbed, yet in my defense, I reacted and knew my legs were free, so I kicked my dad in the face, fled for my life and ran out of the house and never went back.

What just happened? I'm a homeless teen and a mess. I had to figure out what to do and where to go… but this event catapulted me into a season of 'growing up too quickly.' It was a good thing that I was working part-time at a restaurant in the city. My boss graciously offered that I stay at the restaurant's office, which was attached to a windmill. It was perfect! I had a job, a place to stay, a blow-up bed, keys to the restaurant for showering and food, living in the heart of mid-city Wellington, and the freedom to party as much as I wanted.

I never wanted anything to do with my dad and he never wanted anything to do with me, or so I had thought. I was out of control and did not know all the things my parents had gone through, not knowing what their story was and still, I chose to rebel and do my own thing. It seemed as if this type of lifestyle was acceptable, thinking everyone else was doing it... I was wrong.

Mum and dad were living separate lives during this time, and there was talk about possibly divorcing. "Oh yes! Please do!" we siblings would suggest. "You're both better off divorced than married to each other." Years went by and now I'm nineteen– it happens, they finally divorce, and it's said and done.

I remember a time when my siblings and I huddled in a circle and embraced each other, making a pact that wherever we are in the world, whatever we go through and face, that we siblings would promise to love each other, support each other and be there in any way that we can. My brother describes this moment as being the 'relief' from tension.

For most people who experience divorce, it's a tragic event for the parents and kids but you see for us, it was the opposite. There was a sense of independence, the ability to be free from drama, trauma, hatred, and negativity. Our season of living as a family has come to an end. That the dependency of needing our parents was released. No longer could they use us kids as an excuse "we're only together because of you kids, I hate your mother/father." We were finally released from the guilt, burden, and blockage to their happiness. It was as if this moment released us from keeping our parents emotionally captive and in bondage. Finally, we were able to experience this type of relief and although their marriage had ended, the spirit of oppression continued to grow and fester in my life.

Process 5 – Removal - The process of removing the glass from the metal pole that was used to blow requires a special tool

I see that the tool used in this season was the tool of co-dependence. Being freed from obligation and living up to the expectations of our parents and our communities. My siblings and I became independent and grew up quickly at a young age.

I read, "A stronghold can be well developed in our lives, where we fortify a place of negative mindset, and our thoughts have effects on the situation in our lives." God desires that we allow Him to remove the limitations of our minds and challenge the limitations. Let your mind be renewed and transformed. In other words, 'worldview' rejects God and His revelation. As unbelievers, we are naturally conformed to the world (Ephesians 2:1–3). But as believers, we are no longer conformed to this world because we no longer belong to the spirit of this age.'

> Therefore, I urge you, brothers and sisters, in view of God's mercy, to offer your bodies as a living sacrifice, holy and pleasing to God-this is your true and proper worship. Do not conform to the pattern of this world but be transformed by the renewing of your mind. Then you will be able to test and approve what God's will is-his good, pleasing, and perfect will.
>
> Romans 12:1–2 (NIV)

Chapter 6 – Your Warfare

A definition of 'spiritual warfare' is the cosmic war of good vs. evil; its battles are fought daily between God and Satan; between the church and the world's systems; between the Holy Spirit and the lusts of the carnal flesh. In this chapter I can describe my spiritual warfare as being the lies and attacks of Satan.

Now, again the spirit of oppression is heavy and seems like a reality to me, so, I'm still suppressing my emotions with substances and giving into the flesh, drinking my sorrows away and dabbling with drugs. I knew how to be a functioning alcoholic – work by day and drink by night. Mum and dad are separated and before you can officially divorce, you must live separately for two years.

It was 1995, and my father and I are on speaking terms, but it is not 100%. His constant put downs and shaming comments have become bearable because I don't have to live with him anymore – I'm in control of my reactions and responses, but it was in an unhealthy way. A truth I didn't realize was that although I knew how to be bubbly and laugh things off, I'm not happy and my relationships were toxic.

Dad proposes an opportunity for my brother and I to move to Samoa when the divorce is settled. He had decided to return to the islands and establish a family welding business with the funds from selling our childhood home. Hesitantly I agree, but I'm comforted in knowing that my brother will be there with me.

And so, we move to the islands and try to start a new life. The choices are different, and we are acclimatizing to the heat and lifestyle. I felt we didn't have to pursue a career or must have a great job because we are able to live off the land and be contemptuous with the little provision we were satisfied with. But my brother and I are still living the lifestyle of drinking and partying, this has become too much for our dad to bear in Samoa.

Dad is single, divorced, and most likely having to face the shame and tainted reputation he already has with his family. The last thing dad needed was having two of his kids in Samoa, partying and ruining his reputation. Months go by and my brother and dad are having a fight, not just an argument, I'm talking a brawl! Fists and all! This was it for dad... he decided to send my brother back home as soon as he could, the next flight possible. But wait? What about me? Am I to stay back and help dad?

As hard as it was for me to say goodbye to my brother, it wasn't long thereafter that dad had thrown me out of the house and chased me down the streets, throwing beer bottles.

And so, here I am once again, homeless, in Samoa living at the back of the unfinished restaurant that was getting remodeled. Luckily, I was working here as a chef and my boss graciously allowed me to stay there until I could figure out my housing situation.

My aunt, dad's sister, offered to let me stay in their vacant house. Finally, I had a bed to sleep on. I believe it was five to six months before I had got word that mum had flown to Samoa to come find me to take me back home. The reunion with my mum was so special! I cried tears of joy and was relieved that I was rescued from the heartache of feeling unloved by dad once again and excited that I would be reunited with my siblings.

I'm back! I'm back in New Zealand, back in Wellington and you'd think I should be happy right? I'm helping my sister raise her kids, and we siblings are reunited, and yet my sister, brother and I continue to drink and party – we didn't know any different.

It's 1997 and my brother asks "Hey, shall we move to a different city? Let's move to Auckland. We can sleep in the car and take turns sleeping on the mattress at the back vs. the front."

We knew what it felt like to sleep in the car as kids, so we both packed our things and started the twelve-hour drive from Wellington to Auckland. Back in those days, cassette singles were very popular, and we only had the "Return of the Mack" tape. For most of the drive when there was no radio reception, this song was on repeat throughout the journey. I have fond fun memories with my brother and this song. Every time I hear this song, we're reminded of the days we ventured to be homeless in a city we weren't familiar with.

We continued to drink at the local pubs but didn't have to worry about drinking and driving because our 'paddy wagon' was parked outside. My brother is great with his hands and knows how to make anything with wood. He'd built cabinets in the back of the wagon where our pots, pans, clothes, and iron were all stored. The orange curtains would block out the sun and hide us when it was time to sleep. We functioned and it worked for us, and we were surviving out on the streets. We knew where to park and sleep, where the mission center was to eat, how to live from day to day - we were very comfortable and contemptuous.

I'm not sure how we ended up at the YMCA, I believe it was my brother and the connections he had made at the mission center, but we found ourselves as residents of the downtown YMCA Auckland. We met some amazing people who became our friends – other kiwis who like us, traveled to Auckland from another city or people from other countries who were traveling or homeless.

It was here that I met my boyfriend 'Mr. C' who I became fond of. He was a Kiwi, over 6 feet, handsome with red hair and very proper! As I'm finding myself and purpose in life, I'm also changing careers and thinking to myself, my days of parties and sleeping around are done.

We dated for a few years and moved into together, from what I had thought – we fell in love. But this was not the truth for him. You see, I fell pregnant, and his parents encouraged us to both get married and not raise a child out of wedlock. So, we got engaged and started planning the details for our upcoming wedding.

One morning, I awoke to a pool of blood and was rushed to the hospital. The Dr's advised me they needed to perform an ectopic procedure, and that I had an ectopic pregnancy. I was devastated! I had already in my mind, prepared myself emotionally for being a mother, and that the idea of being a mother could somehow straighten me out. I had even chosen names 'Petra' if a girl or 'Nate' if a boy. So, while I'm recovering and emotionally distraught in the hospital, dealing with the truth of having miscarried my first baby, little did I know that my fiancé had taken the opportunity to clear his belongings and move out.

The day came when I was released and had walked into a semi-empty apartment where he said his goodbyes without any explanation and drove away with his brother. I had just lost my baby and my fiancé within the same week.

The feeling I felt must've been how Joseph felt when he was thrown into a pit, betrayed, and sold into slavery. This realization led me to drink more, and I fell into a deep depression of denial. I had lost hope and sense of self-worth and purpose. I even agreed with the comments that were spoken over me – that I was "nothing" I was "useless," that I'm "ugly and fat and that no one would love me."

Looking back, I really appreciate my siblings and their promise to be there for me, especially my brother Gabriel who would always drop what he was doing to visit and loved me in my darkest moments. And as the years went by, I started to make some headway and am coming out of the deep dark depression, even my sense of humor had come back.

Now this next relationship I'm in however, is with a divorced father of two – he is quirky, fun and has a sense of humor. But after two years of living together, his addiction to porn and sex lead to another miscarriage and heart ache because of his unfaithfulness and infidelity – so we split up and go our separate ways.

Now I'm thinking to myself, *I need a change in my life! I need something different!* Although this would have been the perfect time for me to get closer to God and receive my salvation, the world's system is very different and portraits the change as either needing a change of career or place of living.

Dad had met a woman in Samoa, married her, and she became pregnant. Mum was still pursuing her career but now she is saved, having given her life to Christ when Papa died in the USA.

In my next season it's 2005, and I'm working for a company that is in both New Zealand and Australia. I'm promoted and transferred to Sydney, so it's a new country, new beginnings, and opportunities, but do my choices change or is my lifestyle different? Absolutely not!

And so here I am, renting a room in Parramatta, with an acquaintance I had met in New Zealand – I don't really know that much about his history but that he's a nice guy and friendly.

One Friday night, we're out with my work colleagues for happy hour drinks when suddenly he is offended by a comment or situation, then leaves to go home.

I think nothing of it and continue to stay out late. Early Saturday morning, I finally made my way back home and crawled into bed but couldn't help feeling an eerie feeling.

I awoke to my door being opened and saw the silhouette figure of my roommate, "Michael, what do you want?"

His silence was chilling, and I sensed an evilness over him. Michael ran towards my bed, flipped the mattress and bed frame where my body was tossed to the ground like a rag doll, then he proceeded to grab me by my hair and threw me up against the wall and placed his knee down into my neck. Screaming for my life, he was chanting threatening words and the tone of his voice was evil. His grip on my hair was so hard I could feel my hair roots being pulled. This violent attack ended with him in jail and me in the ER.

I had enough! I had enough! The lifestyle of being hurt, violently attacked, drama, trauma… I was done! I was done! I couldn't face life anymore and I had hit rock bottom.

Sitting in the courtroom, he is charged with assault and issued a restraining order. I'm thankful I didn't have to testify as a witness, however the chilling discovery of hearing that Michael was diagnosed as a child with extreme schizophrenia where he confessed, he had thoughts of murdering his parents as he watched them sleep.

When mum had heard her daughter Andie, once again needed to be rescued, she flew over to Australia in my time of need – oh the power of a praying mum works wonders!

"Are you done? Have you finished rebelling? When are you going to learn? Have you had enough?" were the words mum asked me. "You need to repent and ask Jesus into your life. You need to ask for His forgiveness!"

Although mum would always say this to my siblings and I, my ears were finally opened, and I have nothing to lose. But how? Where? Where do I surrender and what do I do? Where do I need to go?

Process 6 – Marking the **neck** of each piece manually is marked, using the tips of the tools to leave an opening where the globe is blown.

> "I have given you the ability to have breakthroughs in your relational situations, through my will and desire for you in situations that would normally break down families or relationships. When you are wounded or hurt by something, your relational cycle does or says, lean into me and I will bring breakthrough into your very being" – Yeshua

> Prophecies, prayers, and declarations – 'Breakthrough' – Shawn Bolz

Chapter 7 – Your Shadows

Process 7 - Sometimes a hemispherical mold is used to speed up the production of parts, in this step, the craftsman, continuously blowing glass mass so that it expands to the limits of the mold of figure.

My long-lost cousin that I hadn't seen since childhood, is 'who' connected me to the new life of knowing Christ. She and her talented children are all worshippers. I called them - 'The Tribe of Judah' and they invited me to go to their church in Liverpool. I remember I had just dropped off mum at the airport and started to head towards the church, not knowing what to expect but was greeted with warm smiles and friendly waves! I had never been to a church that was lively, shaped like an auditorium, and had more than just an organ and guitar! It was my first time experiencing this 'Charismatic' church culture.

When the time came to close the service, the pastor asked if there was anyone in the church that didn't know Jesus to raise their hands and just like that, both my hands were raised, and I was bawling! My questions were answered, "So that's how you give your life! You're invited to respond, and your response is a reaction to your heart being filled with desperation, desire, and hope." And just like that, my journey with God began in such a 'speedily way' –that the only way I can describe these next events as being 'a quickening' or as described above: 'speed up the production of parts'...

Encounter 1:

I joined the New Christian classes and grew closer to

God so that I would have an understanding about praying in tongues, holy spirit fire, words of knowledge and the giftings. In one sitting, we were encouraged to 'fast' for breakthrough and so, I started.

On day three, I started to feel a strong pain near my left ribs, and it was excruciating. After five days of tolerating the pain... I decided to visit the doctor who then proceeded to ask how all this came about. When I mentioned I was on day five of fasting, she gently closed the door and said, "I'm going to do something, and I don't want you to mention me – but I'm a believer and I believe this is a 'spiritual attack' – I'm going to lay my hands on you And pray for you." – she started to rebuke whatever was inside me and was waging war in her prayers! Tears were flowing, as I had never had this type of prayer experience and, for a DOCTOR to put aside her medical profession and declare the name of Jesus – that's HUGE and unheard of. I thank God for her because that night, I was healed in Yeshua's name and was able to sleep on my side.

> Then he put his hands on her, and immediately
> she straightened up and praised God.

> Luke 13:13 (NIV)

Encounter 2:

After 5 months of attending church, the children's pastor had offered me the opportunity to be her assistant. So, I resigned from my job and soon thereafter, became one of the kids' pastor alongside her - I have some amazing fun memories serving in kids' ministry. My joy was being restored and the desire to minister through worship grew passionately – I'm on a journey of trying to discover who I am. Thank you Pastor Alice for believing in me.

Restore to me the joy of Your salvation and sustain me with a willing spirit.

Psalms 51:12 (NIV)

Encounter 3:

Our staff went to the Hillsong conference, and I was blessed to be seated right beside Pastor Henry - a mighty prayer warrior! The message delivered was about identity vs. purpose. When the speaker was emphasizing his key points; I would be reminded of hurtful memories and lies I had believed in. But as each memory surfaced, God would graciously say, "I'm taking these emotions and pain away from you now." ... I could feel the layers of oppression lift – I describe this moment as like an onion being lifted out of the dirty ground then having each layer removed, layer by layer – God was peeling back oppression. Thank you, Pastor Henry, for praying for me during this process.

And they may come to their senses and escape from the snare of the devil, having been held captive by him to do his will.

2 Timothy 2:26 (NIV)

Encounter 4:

Michael called me from an unknown number – the peace of God, that is described 'he will give, and it will never leave us' overwhelmed me with compassion to say to him that I forgave him and that he needed to know Jesus – he hung up. Thank you, Yeshua, for reminding me that love abounds a multitude of sins.

Above all, love each other deeply, because love covers a multitude of sins.

1 Peter 4:8 (NIV)

Encounter 5:

One time in my apartment; I was reading the word and I heard the Holy Spirit say, *call your dad*. I was reluctant and paced the room, battling with God's direction to check in with dad. I remember dialing the number and my hands were shaking, then when I heard Dad answered the phone, I dropped to my knees and started bawling. Dad couldn't piece together who had just called but when I found the strength to start Speaking – all the words that came from me were "totally the Holy Spirit!"

"Dad, Dad, it's Andrea – please forgive me – please forgive me! I've hated you all these years – I've disrespected you and I have rebelled against you. I must let you know that I made choices that have done nothing but bring shame to you and hurt you. Will you forgive me dad – I'm so sorry – will you forgive me?"

My dad on the receiving end was sobbing and began to wail and cried out, "I love you so much my daughter – I'm sorry for hurting you and for not being a good father – there are so many things I've done wrong, and I wish I could change the past. Will you please forgive me, my daughter? Will you please forgive me?"

Asking for **forgiveness** can be tricky if you don't know what to say. Sometimes, people struggle to apologize, so they avoid it instead, worsening the situation. When you ask for forgiveness, it offers the opportunity to repair relationships and correct wrongdoings.

Asking for forgiveness is also an act of **compassion,** helping you and the other person maintain emotional stability. It allows both of you to move on from the past and begin anew. When you're harboring guilt or regret, it can be hard to feel happy and fulfilled.

The good news is that God is the chief restorer, he restores health (Jeremiah 30:17), He restores glory (Haggai 2:9), He restores peace and several other things (Joel 2:25).

Restoration: may He restore unto you everything your family has lost in time past in the mighty name of Yeshua. Just like the process of 'molding to speed up the production of parts' – this is exactly how God works – He will always present an opportunity for us to deal with the matters of unforgiveness, resentment, the 'shadows' we have in our lives. For some, it will happen quickly, while for others this takes time – I guess it's dependent on how much you surrender to Him.

From this night, my nightmares of dad chasing me had finally ended. I dreamt that we were hugging tightly in a crowd of people and we wouldn't let go of each other – God was above us, smiling.

> The Lord delights in those who fear him, who
> put their hope in his unfailing love.

> Psalms 147:11 (NIV)

Chapter 8 – Your Salvation

Process 8 - The mass of hot glass is out of the furnace when it is **cooled** 10°C by second, therefore it is **important to re-heat** to keep taking their viscosity, to continue the transformation process.

Our salvation is the most important process through it all! Knowing who God is and who He can be for you is crucial to your identity in Him and His purposes for your life.

Just as it's described in Process 8 – the cooling process is the encounter process, the refining process, the cooling, and assurance of the Holy Spirit letting us know that we are in His capable hands, and that He alone is in control.

When we understand the sacrifice the Messiah made for us, He will manifest His willingness to reveal more of himself and His will for our lives. It's an attitude of putting God first in your life, even if we find ourselves in a place where we need to be humbled!

Speaking from experience, don't wait for your problems to drive you into a relationship with Yeshua – know that God is gracious, merciful, and desires that we devote our love and attention to Him. If you haven't given your heart to our Messiah, I pray and hope that my story has encouraged you to allow your heart to be opened to receive Him. He will never push Himself on you as He will only allow Himself to be invited into your heart. And once you have decided to follow the Messiah, be fully convinced, and stay decided!

The re-heating process I believe is after accepting Him, we become passionately in love with the Lord, on fire! Full of zeal and our spirits come alive in Him! We're re-heated on the inside because of the hope and trust we have found in the Lord and the transformation will start to take place through our salvation.

> "I have been crucified with Christ; it is no longer I who live, but Christ lives in me…"

> Galatians 2:20 (NIV)

> "For you died, and your life is hidden with Christ in God."

> Colossians 3:3 (NIV)

The first step to being on fire for Yeshua is to make sure you haven't subscribed to a man-centered gospel but rather a Christ-centered gospel. A Christ-centered gospel says, "I am no longer living for myself but for Yeshua." When Christ becomes the center of your life then doing anything for Him won't be a sacrifice, it is your actual life.

Being on fire for God doesn't come automatically, you must intentionally work at it. However, if you leave it up to chance your fire will go out.

> "Therefore, we do not lose heart. Though outwardly we are wasting away, yet inwardly we are being renewed day by day."

> 2 Corinthians 4:16 (NIV)

> "And He died for all, that those who live should live no longer for themselves, but for Him who died for them and rose again."

> 2 Corinthians 5:15 (NIV)

I read a blog that has in my opinion, the best five things that will show you how to keep your fire burning and what you can do to get back on fire for Yeshua:

1. Fully surrender to Christ

The truth is that to come alive to Christ, you first must die to yourself. If you are at the center of your life and are living for yourself, you will find it hard to be on fire for Yeshua. You must get off your throne and let Him sit on it.

2. Focus on Eternity

Eternity is the highest perspective we can have in life. Everything else finds its place and priority when we see things from eternity. If we do not live with eternity pressing into our priorities here on earth, then we'll get easily distracted and caught up living for trivial things – our comforts and pleasures. When difficulties from following Yeshua challenge our quest for comfort and pleasure, then compromising our commitment to Christ won't seem so bad. However, when we see things how Christ sees them, our priorities here on earth change. When we live with heaven's priorities it will cause us to get on fire for God.

3. Feed and fan the flames

The third step to being on fire for Yeshua is to feed and fan the flames of your passion for Yeshua. If you don't, they will easily go out just as a fire eventually goes out if you don't feed and fan it.

These scriptures below show us we need to do, something to maintain our passion and focus for Christ:

Romans 10:17- NIV, "Consequently, faith comes from hearing the message, and the message is heard through the word about Christ."

2 Timothy 1:6- NIV, "For this reason I remind you to fan into flame the gift of God, which is in you through the laying on of my hands,"

Jude 20 -ESV, "But you, beloved, building yourselves up on your most holy faith, praying in the Holy Spirit."

1 Timothy 6:10-12- NIV, "Some people, eager for money, have wandered from the faith and pierced themselves with many griefs. But you, man of God, flee from all this, and pursue righteousness, godliness, faith, love, endurance and gentleness. Fight the good fight of the faith. Take hold of the eternal life to which you were called when you made your good confession in the presence of many witnesses."

4. Find your purpose

With no purpose your life becomes aimless with no reason to be on fire. But when you find and follow your God given purpose it will stir up a fire in you. Our mission is to disciple the nations, and our purpose is to find out how we fit into that and fulfill it with our talents and calling. It's easier to find out your purpose when you are surrendered to Christ, living for eternity, and feeding and fanning the flames of your passion for Christ. When you get connected with your higher purpose it's easier to get on fire for God. If you're not on fire for God, it's probably partly due to you not being connected to your purpose.

5. Fellowship with fired up people

The fifth step to getting on fire for God is to surround yourself with other people who are on fire for God. Fire is contagious, it spreads. All you must do is get around people who are on fire for God and they will fire you up. Then get around other people whose fire has died down and you fire them up! Hopefully, your local church has some people like this and especially the leadership. If the leaders are not fired up, I doubt the people will be.

What kind of believers do you fellowship with? Are they on fire for God or has their fire gone out? What topics dominate their conversations – work, weather, sport, news, themselves – how about Yeshua? How about eternity? How about Kingdom purpose? How about the Word of God?

No matter how far away from God we are, you're always invited to have a personal intimate relationship with Him, and He will always welcome us back. The fire changes us and the trials will rearrange us!

I read "love compels us to accept the integrity of the gift, and to manifest the gift to others. Jesus urges us onward, always believes in us, always hoping for the best, never failing to fight for the fruit we can bear. Love delights in our broken ground – it is deep soil in which He longs to rain down righteousness."
– Living Waters

> Some people, eager for money, have wandered from the faith and pierced themselves with many griefs. But you, man of God, flee from all this, and pursue righteousness, godliness, faith, love, endurance and gentleness. Fight the good fight of the faith. Take hold of the eternal life to which you were called when you made your good confession in the presence of many witnesses.
>
> 2 Peter 3:9 (NIV)

> For it is God who works in you to will and to act in order to fulfill his good purpose.
>
> Philippians 2:13 (NIV)

Chapter 9 – Your Purpose

Process 9: The craftsman is using the **metal plate to support it** and further **expand** the glass to the required diameter of the workpiece.

Fulfilling God's purpose for our life begins with a clean heart – one that loves the Lord and wants to obey Him. Becoming the person God planned us to be requires an intimate relationship with Him and a desire to obey.

As believers, we expect the Holy Spirit to direct us through prayer and scripture, but He also chooses to speak to us in our daily lives either through dreams, audibly or through people. When the Lord visits us and pursues us, He comes for a purpose, and His calls are rare and unexpected. He has a way of making His presence known in our lives, so, let's have an open heart and willingness to be directed by Him.

In 2009, I didn't know the Lord was going to call me to the United States – a close friend had suggested that I consider moving to California and serve at the Los Angeles Dream Center as a volunteer missionary. I remember navigating their website and being inspired by the outreach programs they offered – Skid Row outreach, feeding the homeless, discipleship programs, also backpack giveaways for children of low-income families.

And so, I started filling the application and before I clicked submit, I prayed this prayer "Lord, if this is your will, my heart is willing to go and for confirmation–will you please have me be part of the Back to School Bash! in Jesus's name. Amen."

I'm sure you can relate to these types of prayers – asking for His will to be confirmed with something you're stirred up about... smile.

Submit! It was done and I patiently waited in anticipation for their response – it felt like the longest six months! Finally, the email arrived stating I was accepted and my dreams and goals of ministering in Australia had now shifted to America! I was excited – not knowing what to expect or what the Lord was doing! When I announced to my family that I was preparing to move to the USA – my mum did everything in her power to join me on this journey – and so we went ahead and planned for our trip.

I remember the Lord distinctly saying to me I only needed a one-way ticket for this next season, and that all will be revealed once I arrive. But did He reveal everything? Absolutely not... It was for my own good though, because if you know how the Lord works, He waits to see that our obedience is in line with what He desires we pursue.

An example? During the application process, you are given an opportunity to list the different ministries - in consecutive order that you desire to serve in. I know I had placed numbers in all the outreach programs, that ministers to people on the streets of Los Angeles... but the Lord placed me in the office working in the Corporate Relations Department.

And I struggled for the first few months! I'm away from my family and friends, I'm having to adapt to this new culture and country and constantly say – "No, I'm from New Zealand/ Australia not England" or answer questions regarding vegemite and kangaroos.

But it was during my devotional time with the Lord, when I was in the Chapel crying out to Him asking *why am I here?* I hadn't received my confirmation yet. And in His loving quiet way, He spoke to me clearly with this message...

"When I placed you in the Kids Ministry, you asked what I was doing? When I placed you in the Women's Ministry – you questioned my plans again… but this is what I have planned for you all along – I placed you in Kids Ministry so that your childhood would be restored. I placed you in the Women's Ministry so that your 'womanhood' would be restored. And now that you have grown into the woman of God that I've called you to be, you will be used for loving those who are forgotten, unloved and discouraged. Your giftings will be used to glorify my name and you'll be anointed to preach the gospel to those that are incarcerated and have lost all hope! You will be used to restore identity and deliver my message to them that they are a child of God."

This was the turning point for me in my commitment to Christ! He ignited a fire within me to be passionate about ministering to the men and women that are incarcerated.

Not long after God revealed my purpose, I had a vision that I was in a room full of people whose hands were raised to our Lord, but noticed that they were all men? When I prayed about the dream, I wasn't given any indication of what that meant, so I moved on and continued to serve the Lord in Corporate Relations.

The metal plate mentioned in the process was the support system I was receiving while I was serving at The Dream Center, and the time had come when I was notified that we had to start planning for the Backpack Giveaway, to work on donations, procuring the items, and logistics for this event fun activities etc. "What? Hang on?" I asked my boss "are you saying our department is responsible for this outreach event?"

"Yes" she said, "We're responsible for obtaining donations, financial support, gift cards, stationary items etc. for the kids."

Boy, oh boy did I have the biggest smile on my face! There was my confirmation from the Lord!

"Well, can I suggest that we turn this into a huge fun day!? Not only do we give away backpacks and cut hair, but can we do jump houses, have carnival games, have rides and slides for the kids? Make this a HUGE fun-day event?"

"Research the cost and let me know so that I can present to senior leadership." she said... and from this point on... this was my favorite event to coordinate and opportunity to network with companies to support every year.

The Lord will always provide the support system you need for you to 'expand,' 'prosper,' 'flourish' when you go about His business. How do I know that God thinks you are special? Yeshua died for you! Because of the Father's love for us, He sent His Son to the cross as a sacrifice for our sins. We don't deserve God's care and protection, but thankfully, deservingness isn't demonstrated in His death.

He gifts us with talents and attributes needed to carry out His purposes. 1 Corinthians 12:11. The Lord loves you. If you read His word, this will be a known truth for you, however, we either believe what we read or read what we believe. If there is a truth that we must know, you won't be able to mature until you start serving and make life about others because we are saved to serve!

> Now to him who is able to do immeasurably more than all we ask or imagine, according to his power that is at work within us
>
> Ephesians 3:20-21 (NIV)

Chapter 10 – Your Refining

Process 10: All pieces of glass that have been blown and cooled are rectified and monitored for quality control.

Refining definition: To reduce to a pure state; purify. To remove by purifying. To free from coarse, unsuitable, or immoral characteristics: refined his manners; refined her speaking style. To become free of impurities. To acquire polish or elegance. To use precise distinctions and subtlety in thought or speech.

When I think about these definitions of refining, I'm reminded of the times the Lord has allowed me to experience His peace in situations and the stretching times when facing circumstances out of my control.

After a year of volunteering at The Dream Center, I'm offered an opportunity to come on staff as the Director of Corporate Relations, (hence one way ticket – no going back home) and I'm serving at as volunteer Chaplain at the County Jails and leading worship in some of the various ministries I'm committed too.

And although I'm passionate about serving the Lord, I'm reflecting on the fact that I'm single and my heart is still yearning to be married to someone with the same calling.

The book *Power of a Praying Wife* was handed to me to read. "Andie, I really believe you should read this book because it will help you to prepare your heart - before you become a wife." – and so I did, twice even, three times and more! I rarely read books where I must re-read repeatedly, but this book gripped me - as I'm encouraged to pray for **every area** of his life, even though I didn't know who he would be. Single and not dating, I'm hopeful and anxious to know who this person is!

Now, since I became a believer, the Lord had ministered to me as a woman of God in my singleness – restoring all that was taken from me in my identity as a child, a woman and even renewing my mind as a pioneer for His Kingdom.

And for over ten years I am fully dedicated to the call on my life and focusing on ministry, not fretting about being married or having a husband, and yet, this book gripped me to start thinking of the possibility of being united with a strong man of God.

In 2014, my mum fell violently ill, and we were staying on a floor at the Dream Center that allowed wheelchair access. Every day, I would push mum in her wheelchair to the cafeteria and pass a tall, handsome, six-foot man who would be waiting outside his boss's office to start work at 7 a.m.

"Good morning" We would say as we walked by... was the most our conversation would be for weeks on end, until one day when mum and I were in line at the cafeteria, he approached us asking if he could join us as we waited - niceties and small talk was all I remembered.

My next interaction with him was on our way to church – it was a real struggle having to push mum all the way to Angelus Temple, but he graciously happened to be walking with us and we took turns, pushing mum over cracked sidewalks and busy intersections.

My heart started to become softened towards him, intrigued with wanting to know more about him but also mindful that I am trying to care for mum, and she is to be my priority at this time.

Then, it happened – he asked if we could go out on a date and share a meal... excited and all giddy – I accepted and prayed every day that our courtship would be genuine and centered around God.

"Andie – he is your **husband**." is what mum would murmur every time she saw him. "Eh – mum... stop it... we're only friends right now." But after a few months of dating, the time came for me to fly mum back home to be cared for by my siblings. Grant and I reassured each other that we would wait for time for us to be united – it was the longest few months.

A mother's discernment is something we should never take for granted... speaking of... Grant and I have now been married for seven years. From having dated for nine months, engaged for eight days and married for seven years... God's plans for your life are always to prosper and be aligned with someone with a greater purpose.

I would best describe Grant as a man's man - one who really knows how to minister to fellow men, whether unsaved or saved. He is compassionate and caring, has a big heart and is very friendly. When I had prayed that my husband would be a strong man, I was blessed to be given him... but be sure when you pray that your prayers are specific! You see, Grant has a strong opinion and that is what I guess I'm blessed with, lol.

Our marriage, however, has not been sweet roses of fragrance and rainbows of fulfilled promises! The first six and a half years – Grant has struggled with his identity and his addiction to alcohol. When we first married, we continued to stay at the Dream Center as a married couple in a small 12ft by 12ft studio for two years! Confined in a small place, unable to separate with privacy – we were humbled to appreciate our singleness and spaciousness to one's delight!

God had orchestrated one event to the next where He promoted me to a role that involved helping families and traveling – one door was closed and the other was opened wide – so we moved out from the Dream Center and moved onto our lives outside the walls into the larger city of Los Angeles.

But the accountability and the real-life struggles became a hard reality, and this led to my husband's addiction being amplified x 100! Every day he drank, because on every corner there was a liquor store, and it was exhausting.

I can't count how many times we fought and where the enemy would divide us constantly. We could never be on the same page about anything because of the affliction, condemnation, and the stronghold of his addiction. My mum sadly passed away in September 2020 and as you know, COVID had shut down the ability to travel and see our loved ones. My heart was broken! I had to watch mum be buried through a small computer screen via zoom, then deal with a passed-out husband who would constantly have blackouts.

This struggle was hard to cope with, on so many levels! You see, when your loved one has already been through multiple programs, had done prison time due to his choices that afflicted him – it's hard to love them when their actions are unlovable.

But it was God who continued to minister to me, saying to me that I am part of his deliverance and sobriety – that I cannot give up on the man he has given me to love. Divorce is not the answer – absolutely not! Through thick and thin, till death do us part – I was tempted so many times to leave him – but it was God who would graciously remind me, that the man of God He has created Grant to be, is what I should be focusing on, and be hopeful that the day when he returns to his identity, he will be the man of valor I've always been praying for.

My plea to you as the reader is this, if you have loved ones who are dealing with addition and have lost their identity, DON'T GIVE UP, there is hope in Christ, there is hope in YESHUA! He can restore all that has been robbed and restore identity.

It is now September 2022 and Grant is now sober. He is in the best shape I've ever seen him be in – ever! His wholeness began when he recognized his brokenness and need for redemption.

Those nights of laying hands on my husband and praying while he sleeps, playing soaking worship music when he was tormented with nightmares and terrors, and self-hatred thoughts he had believed in for many years that were destructive, are only now part of his story and our journey together.

> "As iron sharpens iron, so one person sharpens another."
>
> Proverbs 27:17 (NIV)

As a married couple, God has entrusted us to minister together to the male inmates incarcerated at the Federal Prison. His plans and His ways are always greater and higher than ours. Grant's story can be used to glorify His name and bring hope and restoration to those who need to know that God is sovereign and loves you through it all! Marriage should not be complicated though we've had many times of trialing through the desert of complications.

One truth I've discovered having been married to Grant is this – God will always align you with someone who will compliment your gifts and talents – who has a similar calling to love others in a way that places God's glory on display.

Our wholeness begins by recognizing our brokenness. Visualize this – a full length mirror – in one piece that is solid and intact, so that when you reflect the light on it – it can bounce off the mirror and reflect as far back into the room as possible.

Now visualize this – a broken mirror – with cracks and imperfections – it's intact but the shattered lines and broken glass is still able to reflect the light, and you see that all the brokenness from the mirror, will reflect the light in many directions, many light rays, and shapes and quite possible – be reflected in a wider range than of the whole-piece mirror.

In other words, your brokenness – once Christ's light is reflected upon it – is beautiful! It has taken on a new form and shape, and the broken glass has transformation and reversible change. You must accept the changes and evolve, no matter how hard it is.

An identity truth I want to mention – your identity is not found in your addiction, it's not found in other's opinions of you or choices you made, it's not found in the prison walls, or the crime committed, or the lies of the enemy – your identity is found in the word of God! But do you believe the word enough to make decisions upon it? We are and can be, the reflection of God's light, but we're only as good as the reflection.

> Again, Jesus spoke to them, saying, "I am the light of the world. Whoever follows me will not walk in darkness but will have the light of life."
>
> John 8:12 (ESV)

> "No one after lighting a lamp covers it with a jar or puts it under a bed, but puts it on a stand, so that those who enter may see the light.
>
> Luke 8:16 (ESV)

> "But you are a chosen race, a royal priesthood, a holy nation, a people for his own possession, that you may proclaim the excellencies of him who called you out of darkness into his marvelous light."
>
> 1 Peter 2:9 (ESV)

Chapter 11 – Your Calling

Process 11: Then they are placed in the boxes for packing and protecting them from all sides with paper, to prevent the glass breaking.

Have you ever looked back at your past and wandered? 'Lord – I don't know what you're doing but... you know what's best for me and your ways are better...' Of course! We all have wandered. We may not have asked the Lord this question, but we've all been in that situation where in the moment, the events are questionable but when you look back – it's the 'A-ha' moment – that makes a lot of sense!

Well, this chapter is all about your calling and what God has created you to be. It is not a dream job or materialistic things that fulfill a sense of self-worth and status. Today we live in a culture that encourages us to look to our work for a sense of purpose and calling. Work has also become how we define ourselves, that work is no longer about economics, but it's about identity. And today our culture is teaching us that our calling is the same as getting our dream job or doing what we love. But let's reflect on this truth... What is the biblical perspective on our calling?

Now don't get me wrong – work is important, and it is important to God! He gave us work to do from the beginning of time! But the Bible clearly reveals that work is not our central calling.

I read a blog that states, *"Although God has designed each of us for special tasks and assignments, His calling for us is much greater and more soul-satisfying than a summons to work. Before being called to something, we are called to Someone."* So, in other words our primary focus is recognizing that our calling is not about us – but about others.

Packed together with protection, in this season, God has me serving at some amazing places that I believe is a strategic move of God. When our obedience is lined up with His direction, we won't need to worry about things falling into place – He has and always will orchestrate things that we wouldn't be able to do without Him.

A few examples to mention...

Called to Discern: Back in 2011, I was introduced to a place called PIHOP – Pasadena International House of Prayer. Located on Lake Ave, Pasadena California –Pasadena International House of Prayer is the day and night prayer room, inspired by David's tabernacle. They are offering Jesus unceasing adoration, while contending for justice and the power of the Holy Spirit to manifest and bring transformation to every sphere of society.

While I was serving at the Dream Center – every Monday and Saturday, I would visit PIHOP and spend three-four hours soaking in worship, meditating on His word, and drawing prophetic pictures. It was my prayer closet and time of reverence. A friend of mine who I co-lead worship with at the Dream Center, encouraged me to audition to be on the worship team, and so I did.

They have a specific format that is based on the heavenly picture mentioned in Revelation 5, which speaks of the harp and the bowl - worship and prayer integrated together. PIHOP follows this format in the following four ways: Worship with the Word, intercession, prophetic worship, and devotional worship.

Today, every Tuesday from 7p.m. – 9p.m., I lead the Intercession Prophetic Worship set with Team TIRLA – 'Tuesday Intercession Revival for Los Angeles.' Our team prays and worships on matters that are dear to the Father's heart for his people. When I reflect on the people who have been called to be part of this team, every person in the past and present, carries a burden to see the lost saved and the church united. I am proud to say that PIHOP has been an integral part of why I am here in the USA. I remember when I was attending Angelus Temple, God called me to intercede for Los Angeles from the top balcony platform during the services, and as a prayer leader then, I was given favor by leadership to not be interrupted in this closed off section.

And now, in a prayer room placed from the foothills of Los Angeles – this same outpoured calling to partner with the Lord's heart continues. A woman born in New Zealand and saved in Australia with a broken past, has been sent to one of the biggest cities in the world to pray and worship over the City of Angels!

Our intentional prayers and prophetic worship sessions have allowed us to come together as a team and create new songs and sounds. I am excited to have written five prophetic songs! Even if nothing happens with this music or songs written, God is so good and my relationship with Yeshua is much deeper because of the ability to discern His heart and sing about His character.

Another example: **Called to Learn** - is the truth of discovering more about Yeshua the Messiah from a Hebraic understanding. Now although I've been a follower of Christ for seventeen years, I must say that my hunger and thirst for knowing God means more to me now than before, as I study as a student of the Israel Institute of Biblical Studies and follow the teachings of Rabbi Jason Sobel.

I have found that Rabbi Jason unlocks spiritual truths between ancient Jewish wisdom and the New Testament. His teachings have equipped me to discover more about the Messiah as a Jewish man - having those "a-ha" moments! On this journey of discovering more truths about my purpose and God's calling over my life, I believe I'm being taught the traditions and the customs of being a Messianic follower - A Christ follower at high definition!

And lastly - this example: **Called to Serve** - In mid-2021, I really felt the Lord was preparing us to be uprooted and moved to the next season in our life. From initially coming from a 12ft x 12ft room, to a three-bedroom, two-bathroom condo - even though Grant and I were contemptuous, we were surrounded by the temptations of liquor stores in our neighborhood, and it was time to change our environment! We both had prayed that the Lord would bless us with a bigger house, big enough to entertain our family and friends - even own a dog as a companion and be a new addition to our family.

And so, I started packing our things, placing things in boxes, and praying and believing in full faith our prayers will be answered. As we started searching and applying for rental properties for months on end - it was in January 2022 that I was approached by Pastor's Rene and Nora Carrillo from Victory Outreach Van Nuys. They needed a worship leader for their Sunday morning service.

Now this is how the Lord works… the same week that I met Rene and Nora, Grant and I had just placed our application to the realtor for four bedrooms, three bath, 2,200 square foot property earlier that week. When I accepted the opportunity to worship lead at VO Van-Nuys - our application was approved within forty-eight hours!

"You see Andie - because you said Yes - the Lord has blessed you with favor." Pastor Rene confirmed. When the Lord calls us to serve, He will open the doors widely for us to enter without any feeling of obligation. Big doors open with small hinges - don't despise the hinge - it's about grabbing a hold of God's purpose in our lives!

Evidently in this season, I have been called to empower and equip the younger generation to rise up as a tribe of Judah, and to reassure them that all this is possible with God.

We must understand the importance of knowing that worship creates an atmosphere where God "moves in" with His presence and power, drawing people to be touched, healed, forgiven, and saved. The word "worship" appears 201 times through the Bible.

Whatever you've been called to do by God - is your act of worship - bringing adoration to Him and coming alive in Christ because He is equipping you, giving you the grace and anointing to fulfill it. I pray that you will be encouraged by this word and that He be enthroned by your obedience to your calling.

> "But the hour is coming, and is now here, when the true worshipers will worship the Father in spirit and truth, for the Father is seeking such people to worship him".
>
> John 4:23 (CSB)

Chapter 12 –
Your Anointing

Process 12 - Then stored for delivery.

> So, he said, "These are the two anointed ones who are standing beside the Lord of all the earth." So, he said, "These are the two who are anointed to serve the Lord of the earth. Then he said to me, "They represent the two anointed ones who stand in the court of the Lord of all the earth."
>
> Zechariah 4:14 (BSB)

> As for you, the anointing which you received from Him abides in you, and you have no need for anyone to each you; but as His anointing teaches you about all things, and is true and is not a lie, and just as it has taught you, you abide in Him.
>
> 1 John 2:27 (NASB)

> The Spirit of the Lord God is upon me, because the Lord has anointed me to bring good news to the afflicted; He has sent me to bind up the brokenhearted, to proclaim liberty to captives and freedom to prisoners.
>
> Isaiah 61:1 (NASB)

I remember hearing a message from a Pastor from South Africa preach, that his leadership and congregation insisted that he open an orphanage within their community.

He prayed, fasted, and sought the Lord, but didn't feel led to do so. Time passes and the congregation continue to insist that he open this facility, because they knew the need was great - and so he asked the Lord for direction and revelation, for wisdom on the father's heart towards this issue and ability to communicate his response.

The Lord provided him the words to say, and so his message on that Sunday was this: "Although I see the need is great and know we have the finances and ability to open an orphanage, I have NOT been appointed and anointed by God to fulfill this. If I do something without the Lord's appointing and anointing - I can do more harm to the children because of my disobedience. The Lord will always provide the resources and people to fulfill His plans, and I am responsible for seeking His direction and taking on tasks being directed by Him, not to take on tasks out of obligation simply because there is a need!"

His response to his congregation will always remind me to stay the course and seek the Lord's direction, and to experience His peace if it's a 'Yes' and be okay to say 'No.'

I consider myself a visual learner, being able to articulate things when the Lord reveals pictures and images.

And so, a picture that comes to mind is a jigsaw puzzle. We're excited to put all the pieces together because we know what the result should look like, but as you know, during the building process, it takes patience and a steady eye to ensure the colors and shapes match the connections for it to fit and make sense. This is how the Lord has worked in my life and I can only assume He has allowed this to happen in your life too.

He will not give you a piece of the puzzle until things have fallen into place... His timing, His direction, His guidance and, His blessing. When the pieces don't fit, give Him praise and thank the Lord that you recognize there is a situation that can only be completed when perspectives align. Sometimes, we try to fit into someone else's puzzle or allow others to join our own jigsaw, which can ultimately be dangerous if we're not anointed or appointed by God.

Many times, I've seen this happen in the Prison Ministry - where volunteers are so eager to participate and have great intentions, yet after going through a lengthy process of having them cleared into the institution, they either quit when something better comes along, or they don't feel they've been called anymore.

Your anointing and appointment by God are crucial to embrace because without effort or striving, you're able to cause hearts to be moved with compassion and zeal. His loving kindness extends and reaches those with effectiveness and with longevity. His anointing will always draw people to Himself through you.

Now, these past few months I've discovered the truth about what this means for me. You see, my dad, last April, was diagnosed with terminal colon cancer. In his old age of 83, although he knows the Lord and considers himself to be a devoted believer, I see dad is still struggling with unforgiveness... those who have wronged him - even if they have already passed on, unforgiveness towards situations where he cannot find closure and also unforgiveness towards himself.

I traveled to visit my dad with my husband and brothers - and learnt some valuable lessons about applying grace, even when grace is not accepted or appreciated. I can only understand that this is an area that the Lord wanted me to learn about the importance of loving unconditionally, having patience, displaying kindness and exuberance with the fruits of the spirit.

My plea to you is to understand your anointing when poured out to your loved ones, will always be known and shown when it's hard.

Ezekiel 36: 25-27 reads, "Then I will sprinkle clean water on you, and you shall be clean; I will cleanse you from all your filthiness and from all your idols. I will give you a new heart and put a new spirit within you; I will take the heart of stone out of your flesh and give you a heart of flesh. I will put my spirit within you and cause you to walk in my statutes and you will keep my judgments and do them."

A vision I have attached to this verse is imagining a clear vase for flowers, they come in many shapes and sizes, transparent or solid, plastic and glass - this vase represents you! You have been uniquely created and shaped by the master creator who looks upon you and says, "you are good!"

Now, as life happens, we're tainted by sin and poor choices - basically things of this world that are not pleasing and worthy of righteousness. Your identity is robbed and becomes a false truth of what we believe we are, and all these false accusations and situations can be represented by dirt inside the vase.

However, when we accept the Lord into our life, we receive His living water and His ways and thoughts towards us start to break down the dirt and mix with these untruths. Things become exposed within us, and we know that we need to have more of God for it to surface! That's why the more we receive His living water, the more the dirt begins to surface, mixing and turning within us.

As we continue receiving His water, slowly and eventually these false identities overflow out of our spirit and are replaced by Him and His thoughts towards us. More of Him, less of us! Now we know we will never be perfect - only Yeshua will ever be this perfect example - so yes of course there will always be residue within us...

But He will give you purpose, visions, dreams, and gifts to fulfill these - what you do with these gifts is your gift to Him.

And so, in closing - the packaging of the anointing are simply these steps:

- **I thought it** - *when God gives you a dream, it is always attached to purpose and promises. This is known as a revelation of truth that we can't and won't let go of. Continue to pray and seek the Lord for confirmation for this dream... it will be confirmed through His peace and Shalom!*

  Jeremiah 29:11 – NLT, "For I know the plans I have for you declares the Lord. Plans to prosper and not to harm, plans for a hope and a future."

- **I caught it** - *When this dream is confirmed, you'll find yourself throwing ideas, pros and cons then looking into it then going beyond it. When it's a God given dream, the door will open and be presented without your help. Let it happen and let Him be the God who provides opportunities.*

  Revelation 3:8 – NLT, "I know all the things you do, and I have opened a door for you that no one can close. You have little strength, yet you obeyed my word and did not deny me."

- **I bought it** - *When you embrace the direction and revelation - there is always a price to pay, maybe a closed door of unnecessary pursuits or relationships that may hinder or prevent you from really fulfilling God's divine plan. Talk is free but pursuing the calling takes risks - be prepared to be equipped for God's abundance - even if we don't see it or believe it could happen - claim it as a promise being fulfilled!*

  2 Timothy 3:17 – ESV, That the man of God may be complete, equipped for every good work."

- **I sought it** - *No talking out of it - pursuing it thanking God for the desire and for preparing you for receiving it*

Psalms 34:4 -NIV, I sought the Lord, and He answered me; He delivered me from all my fears.

- **I got it** – *You're now there – but you must remain faithful with what the Lord has entrusted you to look after and manage. The enemy comes to steal, kill, and destroy and if we're sidetracked, become envious of others or have a sense of pride thinking we did this ourselves, he will humble us – it is better to stay humble than be humbled by God!*

1 Peter 5:5 - NIV, "God opposes the proud but shows favor to the humble."

Matthew 25:23- BSB, "Well done, good and faithful servant! You have been faithful with a few things; I will put you in charge of many things. Enter the joy of your master!"

- **I taught it** – *there is no success without a successor. With all that the Lord has entrusted you, equipped you with and poured out into you, He desires that you go and make disciples of all nations, maybe even mentor someone or teach someone. As a mentor, you serve as a model and trusted listener. You also prove that you rely on the Holy Spirit to provide insight, impart wisdom and direction for others, and that you can influence others and change lives through the modeling process... So, my question to you is, who are you mentoring? And who is mentoring you?*

1 Corinthians 11:1- NIV, "Follow my example as I follow the example of Christ."

My prayer is that you see how God can use anyone to be a minister of light for all to see. He will equip and empower you to fulfill His plans - He will also send people to partner with you to ensure that it is fulfilled.

Imagine a lantern burning and placed on the floor in a room full of people... who can see the lantern? Only those that are near the lantern. People can see the light reflecting but only those close to the lantern can see the lantern, and yet, when you continue being a light for Yeshua and remain obedient, your light will be lifted high above the crowds and placed on a pedestal for all to see. The light and lantern haven't changed, just the positioning of it! He does the promoting and He does the lifting, all you need to do is keep the light and flame burning as a man and woman of valor for our King!

God bless you and all you do for our King! I pray for protection, equipping, provision and anointing to be released over you and your purpose - in His name - Yeshua!

Agape... In His Service

CPSIA information can be obtained
at www.ICGtesting.com
Printed in the USA
BVHW071914130223
658422BV00012B/151